Soccer
Superwomen

By James Buckley, Jr.

The
Child's
World
www.childsworld.com

Published in the United States of America by The Child's World®
P.O. Box 326 • Chanhassen, MN 55317-0326
800-599-READ • www.childsworld.com

ACKNOWLEDGMENTS

The Child's World®: Mary Berendes, Publishing Director

Produced by Shoreline Publishing Group LLC
President / Editorial Director: James Buckley, Jr.
Designer: Tom Carling, carlingdesign.com
Cover Art: Slimfilms
Copy Editor: Beth Adelman

Photo Credits
Cover—Main: Getty Images; Insets: Wire Image, Getty Images (2)
Interior—Getty Images: 5, 7, 9, 10, 14, 20, 24, 26; Wire Image: 8, 13, 16, 18, 21 (2), 23, 29.

LIBRARY OF CONGRESS CATALOGING-IN-PUBLICATION DATA

Buckley, James, 1963–
  Soccer superwomen / by James Buckley, Jr.
     p. cm. — (Girls rock!)
  Includes bibliographical references and index.
  ISBN 1-59296-750-7 (library bound : alk. paper)
 1. Women Soccer players—Biography—Juvenile literature. 2.
Soccer for women—Juvenile literature. I. Title. II. Series.
  GV944.9.A1B83 2006
  796.334082'0922—dc22
                                    2006009023

CONTENTS

AMERICAN Heroes

Soccer might not be America's number-one sport, but even so, America's women soccer players are some of the best in the world!

Before she stopped playing in 2005, Mia Hamm was the top women's star in the world for ten years. Mia was only 16 when she first played for the U.S. national team. In college she helped her

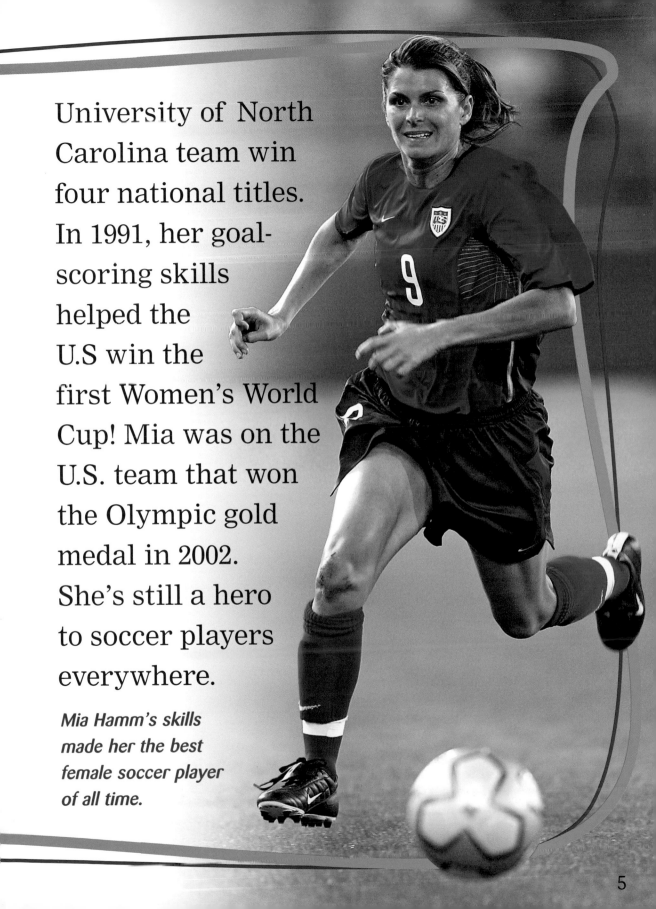

University of North Carolina team win four national titles. In 1991, her goal-scoring skills helped the U.S win the first Women's World Cup! Mia was on the U.S. team that won the Olympic gold medal in 2002. She's still a hero to soccer players everywhere.

Mia Hamm's skills made her the best female soccer player of all time.

Helping Mia score many of her goals was a small and super-fast **forward** named Tiffeny Milbrett. Tiffeny is an expert **dribbler** and great passer. Her speed makes it hard for the other team to follow her. She can always find the right teammate to pass the ball to.

Tiffeny helped the U.S. team win the Women's World Cup in 1991. They won it again in 1999. In 2006, Tiffeny scored her 100th goal for the U.S. Only four other women have scored that many.

Tiffeny, who grew up in Oregon, also has played for pro teams in Japan and Sweden.

Score! Tiffeny celebrates with her teammates after scoring her 100th goal for the U.S. team.

Can't catch me! Kristine Lilly has great ball skills, and she never quits. She has almost never had to come out of a game.

Kristine Lilly has played in more **international** soccer games than any player—man or woman. Through 2005, she had been in 300 games! Her all-around skills and hard work have made her a huge part of U.S. women's soccer.

In 1999, Kristine saved the day for the U.S. in the World Cup final. Near the end of the game, she **headed** away a shot by China just before it went in the goal! The U.S. went on to win that game.

Awesome Akers

Before Mia Hamm, Michelle Akers was considered to be the best women's player of all time. Tall and strong, she was captain of the 1991 U.S. team that won the first World Cup.

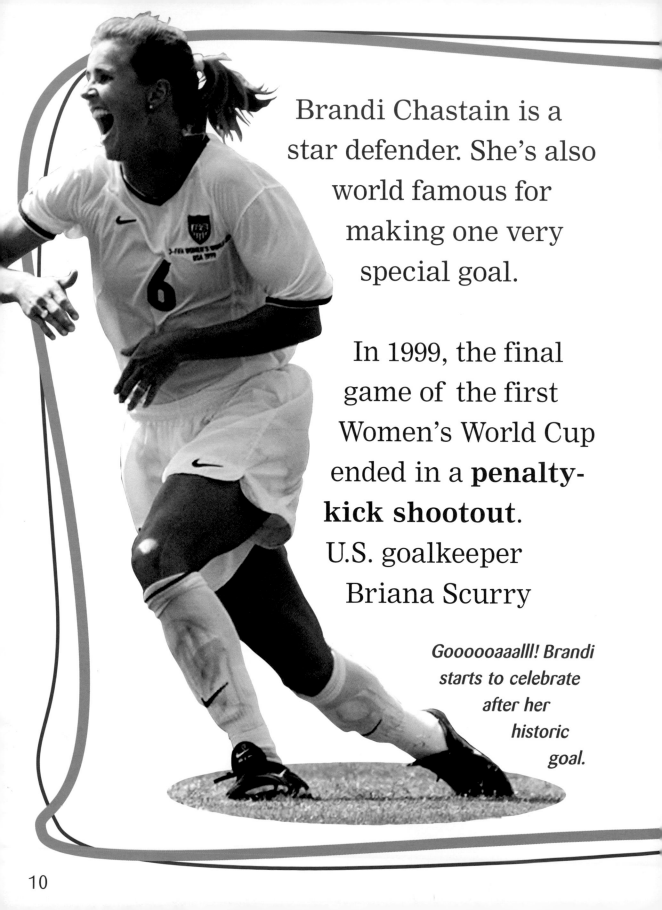

Brandi Chastain is a star defender. She's also world famous for making one very special goal.

In 1999, the final game of the first Women's World Cup ended in a **penalty-kick shootout**. U.S. goalkeeper Briana Scurry

Goooooaaalll! Brandi starts to celebrate after her historic goal.

stopped one shot by China. If the U.S. team made its next shot, they would win.

Brandi stepped up and banged home a left-footed shot. The fans at the stadium in Los Angeles went crazy! Brandi led a huge celebration on the field. Her spirit and energy were a big part of her success.

The women in this chapter set a great example for countless young players. Now let's meet some of the rising stars they inspired.

2

STARS OF THE
Future

12

Today's U.S. women's soccer team has a lot to live up to. The good news is that with players like Abby Wambach, more success is sure to come. Abby is one of the top **strikers** in the world.

In 2003, Abby scored 31 goals! Only one American woman has scored more goals in a single year— Michelle Akers, with 39 in 1991. In 2004, Abby's goal against Brazil gave the U.S. the Olympic gold medal. In 2003 and 2004, Abby was U.S. Women's Player of the Year.

OPPOSITE PAGE
As a top scorer, Abby Wambach always draws a crowd. Here she fights off Brazilian defenders.

Like Mia Hamm and Abby Wambach, Shannon McMillan has made her mark around the goal. She has played in more than 175 international matches, scoring more than 60 goals. In 2002, she led the U.S. team with 17 goals. Her biggest scoring burst came at the 2002 Algarve Cup in Portugal, when she scored seven of the U.S. team's eight goals.

In 2001, Shannon was among many top players who helped start the WUSA, a

When two national soccer teams play a game—or match, in soccer language—it's called an "international."

WUSA stood for Women's United Soccer Associaion.

14

Here's Shannon in the uniform of the San Diego Spirit, one of the teams in the short-lived U.S. women's pro soccer league.

women's pro soccer league. It only lasted three seasons, but it was a great experience for America's top players. Shannon twice led her team in scoring.

Most of the players we've met so far are great goal-scorers. Briana Scurry is a great goal-stopper. She's the longtime goalkeeper for the U.S. national team.

Got it! Briana Scurry makes a save in front of a charging Chinese player.

Briana is always ready for action. Being a goalie takes **concentration**. Nothing happens for long periods, then all of a sudden, you're in the spotlight!.

She first played with the national team in 1994. She has started more games for the U.S. than any other keeper. In 1999, she was named to the World Cup All-Star Team after allowing only three goals during the games. She was the keeper on the U.S. team that won the 1996 Olympic gold medal.

Shannon Boxx started her national-team career with a bang, scoring goals in her first three games. She burst onto the scene during the 2003 World Cup, scoring twice and earning a spot on the World Cup All-Star team.

Shannon is now a key midfielder on the U.S. team. After her 2003 success, she was the most valuable player of the Algarve Cup, which the U.S. won in 2004. She then helped the U.S. win the gold medal at the 2004 Olympics in Australia.

Shannon grew up in California, but her soccer skills have taken her all over the world.

Powerful Shannon is hard to stop when she wants to shoot.

Two young stars are looking to continue the U.S. team's success. At Santa Clara University, Aly Wagner was named college soccer's top player in 2001. She joined the U.S. team in 1998 and later helped the U.S. win Olympic gold in 2004.

A great dribbler, Aly (left) is not afraid to go up for head balls when she has to!

Aly's greatest skills are dribbling and passing. She is one of the best ballhandlers the U.S. has ever seen.

Heather Mitts will be a top defender on U.S. teams in the future. She helped the University of Florida win the college title in 1999, and played in the Olympics and in the WUSA.

Practicing with the great dribblers on the U.S. team has made Heather an even better defender.

Ace Reporter

Heather's a great soccer player, and she puts her knowledge to use off the field, too—as a television reporter covering sports events (especially soccer games).

AROUND THE World

Soccer is the world's most popular game, so it isn't surprising that there are outstanding women players in action all over the globe. Let's meet some of the very best.

Germany's Birgit (BEER-ghit) Prinz has been named the top women's player in the world—twice! She's a powerful, high-scoring forward.

Here's Birgit doing what she does best— getting the ball past the goalie (right) for another goal.

In 2003, she led the German team to its first World Cup championship. She was named the most valuable player of the tournament.

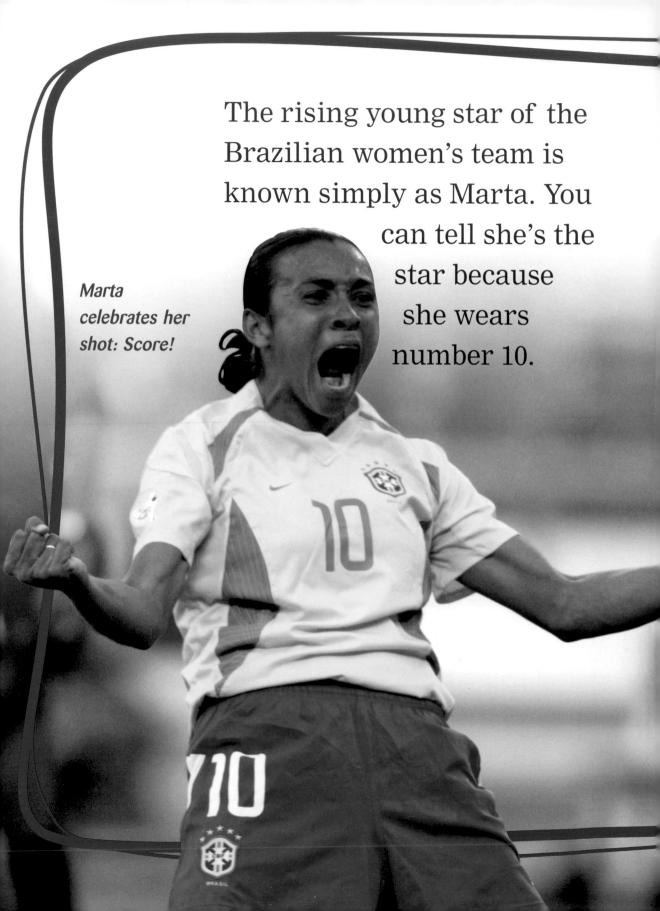

The rising young star of the Brazilian women's team is known simply as Marta. You can tell she's the star because she wears number 10.

Marta celebrates her shot: Score!

That jersey number has a lot of meaning in Brazil, where soccer is the number-one sport. Péle, one of the most famous men's players of all time, wore it. In the 1990s, it was worn by another men's star, Rivaldo.

Marta has continued their **legacy**. She scored six goals to help Brazil win the 1999 Under-19 world title. Then she helped Brazil win gold in the 2003 Pan Am Games. She's still looking for World Cup success.

A legacy is something left behind by someone who has died or has retired from a career or sport.

The popularity of women's soccer is rising fastest in Asia. The largest country in Asia—and the world—is China.

Sun Wen has starred on the Chinese national team for 15 years.

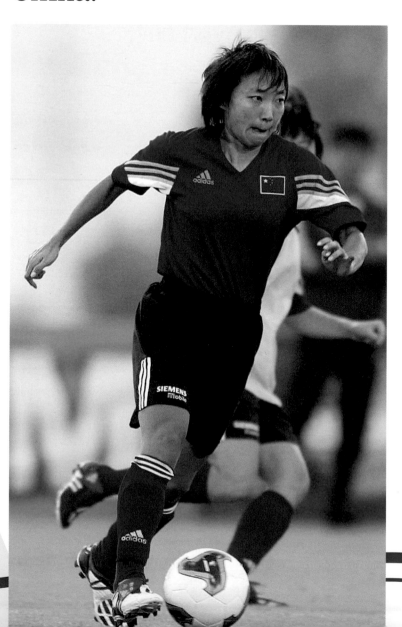

For the past ten years, China has had one of the top women's teams in the world. They won the World Cup in 2003 and will host the tournament in 2007.

Leading the way for China is the dazzling dribbler Sun Wen. In the 1999 World Cup, China lost to the U.S. in the final, but Sun Wen was named the top player for scoring seven goals in six games. Though she will be a **veteran** at the 2007 World Cup, Sun Wen hopes to lead her team to victory at home!

Europe has always been a center of world soccer. On the women's side, a pair of Scandinavian nations— Sweden and Norway—join Germany as Europe's best.

Norway is led by forward Dagny (DAG-nee) Mellgren. In 1999, she scored against Japan as Norway finished fourth in the World Cup.

In 2000, Dagny had her finest success. At the 2000 Summer Olympics final, Norway battled the mighty U.S. team. The game went to overtime.

Dagny's height and great speed make her a goal-scoring powerhouse.

Dagny hammered home a goal to capture the title!

Who will be the next great woman soccer player? You?

GLOSSARY

concentration   the ability to pay close attention for a long period of time

defenders   a position in soccer usually played near a player's own goal

dribbler   a player who is very good at dribbling, or moving the ball along with small taps of each foot

forward   a position in soccer usually played near the other team's goal

headed   hit the ball with the forehead—a way of passing or shooting the ball in soccer

international   having to do with relations between countries, such as soccer games played between two national teams

legacy   what someone leaves behind after they leave a place or after they die

midfielder   a player whose position is between the forwards and defenders

penalty-kick shootout   a contest, in which teams switch off kicking 12-yard shots, held after a soccer game is tied after the regular play of the game

strikers   players whose specific job is to score goals

veteran   in sports, someone who has been playing for many years

FIND OUT MORE

BOOKS

Mia Hamm
by Robert Schnakenberg
(Chelsea House, New York) 2000
A veteran sportswriter shares the biography of the greatest female soccer player ever.

Women's Soccer Scrapbook
by Jill Potvin Schoff
(Somerville House, Toronto, Ontario) 2000
This book takes an inside look at the U.S. team that won the 1999 Women's World Cup, including a foreword by player Kristine Lilly.

WUSA Girls' Guide to Soccer Life
by WUSA Stars
(Cool Springs Press, Nashville, TN) 2003
Check this book out for tips from top pro players in the WUSA. It includes a DVD with highlights of WUSA play.

WEB SITES

Visit our home page for lots of links about women's soccer:
www.childsworld.com/links

Note to Parents, Teachers, and Librarians: We routinely check our Web links to make sure they're safe, active sites—so encourage your readers to check them out!

INDEX

JAMES BUCKLEY, JR., has written more than 45 books on sports for young readers. He has written about baseball, basketball, football, soccer, and the Olympics, among others. He has played soccer since he was a kid, but he's pretty sure that all the women in this book could get by him with no problem!